For Peter, with all my love   A.S.
For Federica   A.R.

Text copyright © 2007 Andrea Skevington
Illustrations copyright © 2007 Angelo Ruta
This edition copyright © 2007 Lion Hudson

The moral rights of the author and illustrator
have been asserted

A Lion Children's Book
an imprint of
Lion Hudson plc
Wilkinson House, Jordan Hill Road,
Oxford OX2 8DR, England
www.lionhudson.com
ISBN: 978-0-7459-4982-6

First edition 2007
10 9 8 7 6 5 4 3 2 1

The Bible retellings are based on the corresponding
passages in the Good News Bible and the Holy Bible,
New International Version. The Good News Bible is
published by The Bible Societies/HarperCollins
Publishers Ltd, UK © American Bible Society 1966,
1971, 1976, 1992. The Holy Bible, New International
Version is copyright © 1973, 1978, 1984 International
Bible Society. Used by permission of Zondervan and
Hodder & Stoughton Limited. All rights reserved. The
'NIV' and 'New International Version' trademarks are
registered in the United States Patent and Trademark
Office by International Bible Society. Use of either
trademark requires the permission of International Bible
Society. UK trademark number 1448790.
The Lord's Prayer (on page 31) from Common
Worship: Services and Prayers for the Church of
England (Church House Publishing, 2000) is
copyright © The English Language Liturgical
Consultation, 1988.

A catalogue record for this book is available
from the British Library

Typeset in 15/19 Venetian 301 BT
Printed and bound in China

THE STORY OF
JESUS

Andrea Skevington

Illustrated by Angelo Ruta

LION
CHILDREN'S

Contents

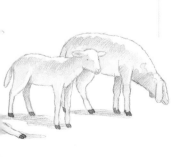

Introduction

The most ancient copies of the Gospels that exist today are written in Greek. This ancient language was commonly spoken throughout the Roman empire.

JESUS IS THE ONE whose life and teachings are at the heart of the Christian faith.

He was a Jew who lived some 2,000 years ago in the traditional homeland of the Jews, on the eastern shore of the Mediterranean Sea. He was raised in a small town among the hills and learned the family trade, becoming a builder and carpenter. Then he became a travelling preacher. He gathered a popular following until the authorities objected to his teaching and conspired to have him put to death.

His life could easily have been forgotten but for the handful of devoted followers who had faith in his teachings. They proclaimed their belief that death had not been able to claim him – that God had raised him to new life and lifted him up to heaven. In this way, they said, Jesus had opened the way for anyone to be part of God's kingdom – the kingdom of heaven.

At this time, the land of the Jews was part of the vast Roman empire. They were able to use the roads and shipping routes of the empire to travel far and wide, spreading their message. Many people who had never met Jesus came to believe all they said. They wanted to know all that Jesus had taught from the people who had actually witnessed the events of his life and death.

But as the years went by, the growing band of Jesus' followers knew they could not rely on these witnesses for ever. They needed a record of Jesus' life that would last through the centuries. Among the accounts of Jesus' life that were written, four were acknowledged to be the most important and they were eventually included in the collection of writings the Christians call the Bible. These accounts are known as the Gospels – from words meaning 'good news', and they are named after the people who are credited with writing them: Matthew, Mark, Luke and John.

Each of the Gospels is different. The Gospel of Mark was probably written around 65–70 CE in the city of Rome, at the heart of the empire. At one time, the emperor Nero was treating the Christians very cruelly, and the book emphasizes that no one need doubt their faith because Jesus really was from God: God's son and God's chosen king – the Messiah, the Christ. According to tradition, Mark was the John Mark who travelled around the empire with two of Christianity's first missionaries, Paul and Barnabas.

The Gospel of Luke may have been written next, perhaps between 70 and 85 CE. Luke was a doctor and a non-Jew, or Gentile, and also accompanied Paul. He wrote his Gospel in a way that other non-Jews who might not know much about Jewish customs could easily understand.

The Gospel of Matthew, by contrast, was written for Jewish people. It takes every opportunity to point out how, in Jesus, the words of the Jewish prophets have come true. The name Matthew is linked with one of Jesus' closest followers, the twelve disciples. It was probably written around 80 CE.

John is also the name of one of the disciples. The Gospel that bears his name was probably completed a few years after the others. Although clearly writing about the same Jesus, it records many different stories and sayings from the other three Gospels.

This book has selected some of the most important stories from each of the Gospels and retold them faithfully to portray Jesus as his followers knew him.

The Beginning

JOHN 1:1–5,
9–14, 18

IN THE BEGINNING was the Word.
   Before the dawn of time —
before the earth, the waters and the stars —
the Word was there with God, was God.
In the beginning, there was simply nothing else.

But then, the Word spoke out into the empty blankness,
and life and light were unleashed.
The universe spun into song, opening like an oasis
   of flowers in the morning light.

8

This Word, this light of the world, shines in the darkness —
cold, smothering shadows where nothing can grow — and
darkness recoils at its touch. It does not understand a light
    that cannot be put out.

This Word, the One who was there from the beginning,
became flesh and blood, and chose to make a home
with us in this fragile, changing world.

And we have seen the glory of this One and only
with our own eyes — shining with life and light.
We have seen the very One who came to us from the Father.

No one has ever been able to see God, but this
Jesus, the One and only, who was there
in the beginning, has made God known.

Mary and the Angel

LUKE 1:26–56

IN THE HIGH COUNTRY above the Sea of Galilee nestled the hill town of Nazareth. Here lived Mary, who was engaged to Joseph. One day, something astounding happened. An angel was sent to her with a message.

'Good morning! You are truly honoured! God is with you,' Gabriel began.

'What can this mean?' Mary gasped. But the angel spoke softly to her.

'Mary, don't be afraid. God has chosen you for something wonderful. You will have a child, Jesus. He will be great, and his kingdom will never end...'

The angel's words were full of bright promises, but Mary was troubled.

'I don't understand. Please – how can this be? I am not yet married.'

'The Spirit of God will overshadow you, and your child will be holy, the Son of the Most High,' the angel replied.

'Even your cousin Elizabeth is now in her sixth month – and everyone thought she would never have a child! For with God, nothing is impossible.'

Mary's head was spinning. She paused, looking at the angel, steadying herself.

'Yes, I see. I am ready. Let it be as you say.'

The angel met her gaze, then slipped out of sight.

Mary grabbed a few clothes and hurried to the hill country where Elizabeth lived. She had to talk to Elizabeth – the only one who might understand.

And when Mary burst into her cousin's home, calling Elizabeth's name, the older woman came to greet her.

'My baby leapt for joy at the sound of your voice!' Elizabeth said.

As for Mary, these words soared from her heart like the rising of a lark on a spring day.

Mary's song of joy is said or sung by Christians today. It is often called the Magnificat.

*'My spirit dances before God,
my heart is overflowing with joy!
God did not mind my humble birth
when he chose me. Now, and in all
the years to come, I will be called
blessed by God for ever.'*

How much the two women had to talk about!
They were together for three months, giving each
other courage and help and love. And after Elizabeth gave
birth to John, who was to be John the Baptist, Mary went
home, ready for what was to come.

The Birth of Jesus

LUKE 2:1–7

THE GREAT ROMAN EMPIRE was at the height of its powers. Orders from the emperor himself were being carried to its furthest corners, including Nazareth.

'Caesar Augustus has spoken! All people are to return to their home towns to be counted!' proclaimed the messengers.

Mary and Joseph reluctantly packed the few things they could carry, and set off on the long road south from Nazareth to Bethlehem, the city of David. For Joseph could trace his family back through the centuries to King David himself, the simple shepherd boy who became the great king of the Jews.

And so they travelled back to Joseph's family town. The roads were busy, full of jostling crowds complaining about Roman occupiers and their taxes. Mary and Joseph travelled more slowly, as it was nearly time for Mary's baby to be born. They rested whenever they could, and Mary shut her eyes to picture the angel who had visited her, remembering those bright promises.

At last, they reached Bethlehem — but the crowds had arrived before them. There was no room anywhere, not even at the inn. Joseph asked everyone his family knew, until at last they were offered a stable. Joseph led Mary there sadly — it was hardly his first choice.

Mary settled down on the straw. The noise and bustle seemed to slip away, and all that mattered was the coming child. And so it was that Mary's baby was born in a stable, wrapped up tightly in swaddling bands, and laid in the sweet-smelling hay of the manger.

Mary did not notice the dirt, or the rough mud walls. She and Joseph only had eyes for the newborn child — the precious gift that had been given into their care. They had never seen a baby so perfect, so beautiful.

Jesus' birth in a stable is a reminder to Christians that he cared for the poor and the homeless.

The Shepherds and the Angels

LUKE 2:8–20

Angels are often depicted praising God with the same musical instruments that the Jews used in their worship.

ON THE NIGHT Jesus was born, shepherds were awake in the nearby hills, huddled in their cloaks against the biting wind, keeping watch over their sleeping sheep.

Suddenly, one of the shepherds rose to his feet.

'Look!' he called to the others. They stood, staring, as bright shining light enfolded them. And at its heart, they could see something that took their breaths away.

'An angel!' they cried, terrified, and fell down to the ground.

'Don't be afraid! You are the first to hear wonderful news — news to make the whole world sing for joy,' said the angel.

'Go down into Bethlehem, David's city, and look for the newborn king. You will find him wrapped in swaddling bands and lying in a manger. It will be a sign to you that you have found the one you seek.'

Then, above the bleak, cold hillside, the wide sky burst with light, and a host of angels appeared, scattering their glory over the stony fields. The night was full of song.

'Give glory to God in the highest heavens,
And on earth, peace!'

Suddenly, the darkness closed in again, and all was quiet.

'Come on, let's go!' called a shepherd, already bounding over the rocks and down the hills. 'What are you waiting for? Let's go and see this amazing thing God has told us about!' So off they went, leaving their sheep behind.

And then, they found the stable, just as the angels had said. They found Mary, and Joseph, and a newborn baby, wrapped in swaddling bands and lying in a manger.

The shepherds ran through Bethlehem bursting with joy, telling everyone all they had seen and heard that night. As for Mary, she treasured up all these bright memories, keeping them safe in her heart.

The Coming of the Wise Men

MATTHEW 2:1–15

IN A LAND TO THE EAST of Bethlehem, scholars had been watching a bright new star. They studied its position and pored over their charts with rising excitement, for it could mean only one thing: a great king had been born to the Jews. And so they set off to follow the star.

They arrived in Jerusalem, the great city of the Jews, and began to ask questions. 'Where is the one who has been born king?'

'A new king? Here? What can they mean?' King Herod was troubled by their words, and he gathered together experts in the Jewish laws and prophecies.

'Well, where will the king of the Jews be born?' he roared.

'Bethlehem, sir.'

Herod drummed his fingers on his throne, hatching a terrible plan.

That night, he invited the wise men to the palace. 'Go to Bethlehem and search for the new king,' he said. 'Don't give up until you find him. Then, I'll come and worship him too.' But in his heart, he intended to kill the child.

The wise men set off, and once more followed the bright star. It led them to the place where the child was. They went inside, saw Jesus with his mother, Mary, then bowed low to the dusty floor, and worshipped him. Then, as they unpacked their astonishing gifts, Mary gasped. There was gold, fit for a king; frankincense, an offering of worship; and myrrh, to prepare a body for burial. This king would be remembered for his death, as well as his life.

As the wise men slept, they were troubled by strange dreams warning them about Herod. So they took a different route home, keeping well away from Jerusalem. Joseph, too, had been warned in a dream, and he and his family fled to Egypt, as refugees in fear of their lives. They only returned to Nazareth after Herod's death.

Because Matthew's Gospel names three gifts, it is traditional to show three wise men.

The Boy Jesus

LUKE 2:42–51

Mary was anxious about her son even though twelve marked the beginning of adulthood.

WHEN JESUS WAS TWELVE years old, his family took the road south from Nazareth to Jerusalem, as they did every year. They went to celebrate the festival of Passover – when the Jews remember their rescue from Egypt, and the parting of the Red Sea. The whole community set off together, laughing and talking as they travelled, sharing food and firelight by night. And when the great feast was over, they set off for home again, full of stories about all they had seen and done in the great city.

Then, as night fell, Mary grew uneasy.

'Have you seen Jesus?' she asked his friends one by one.

'No – we thought he was with you!'

Mary felt a knot of fear tighten inside her.

'He'll be all right,' said Joseph. 'He's nearly grown up now. We'll soon find him.' So they hurried back, retracing their steps.

'He could be anywhere – look at the crowds!' Mary was pale and drawn, but Joseph held her hand tight, and pressed on. They searched for three long days and nights. Finally, they went to the Temple – there was nowhere else to turn.

And there Jesus was, sitting among those who taught the Jewish faith, with a sparkle in his eyes and questions on his lips. Everyone was amazed that one so young had such understanding of the ways of God. How at home he looked in that place!

But Mary burst out, 'Son, how could you do this to us? We've been out of our minds with

worry — we've turned the city upside down looking for you!'

'But... surely you knew I'd be here? This is my Father's house...'

At first, his words seemed like nonsense to them. But, as they made the journey home, Mary dwelled on all he had said, keeping the memory safe in her heart.

The shady colonnade of the Temple courtyard was where the Jewish teachers would discuss the faith.

Good News!

MARK 1:1–13

John the Baptist's hair and clothing marked him out as a prophet, or holy man.

IT WAS NEARLY TIME for Jesus to begin his work. But first of all, a messenger came to prepare the way. His name was John, and he lived in the desert, dressed in rough clothes made of camel hair. All he ate was locusts and wild honey – there were no luxuries for him. He told people to turn their lives around, stop doing wrong, and be baptized as a sign of their new beginning.

And people came in droves to hear him preach: city types from Jerusalem and country people from surrounding Judea alike. They flowed out into the heat of the desert, hanging on his every word. He stood in the River Jordan, baptizing all who were moved by his words and wanted to change.

'This is just the beginning!' he said. 'You'll see. There is someone on his way who's truly great. I'm not even good enough to do up his sandals! All I've done is baptize you in water – washed you on the outside. He'll baptize you with the Holy Spirit – wash you from the inside out.'

Just then, Jesus came out of the crowds to be baptized by his cousin John. The moment he came up from the water, he saw the sky rip open, and the Holy Spirit come down on him like a dove. A voice filled the air:

'You are my Son, the one I love, my pride and joy!'

Immediately the Spirit sent Jesus out alone, deeper into the desert, where he was tempted by the Devil for forty days. He shared the wild places with the desert fox and the lizard, the beetle and the hawk. And flights of angels took care of him.

In the parched wilderness, Jesus dedicated himself to living for God.

The Work Begins

LUKE 4:14–37

When he became a preacher, Jesus moved to Capernaum. He taught both out of doors by the lake and in the synagogue.

JESUS BEGAN HIS WORK. He was full of God's spirit, and when he spoke, everyone knew they were hearing something astounding. Everyone listened to him, except for the people of Nazareth, where he had grown up. There, they would not hear his words. So he went to Capernaum, by the Sea of Galilee, where Simon the fisherman lived. It was the sabbath, the holy day, when no work was done. The fishing nets were hung up to dry, the ploughs were still, and the cooking fires were cold. Everyone was going to the synagogue to worship and hear the rabbis, the teachers, read and explain the holy scriptures. A new voice was always welcome, and so Jesus was asked to speak. His words astonished everyone. They were so fresh and vivid – so powerful.

Then there was a disturbance.

'It's him again, isn't it?'

'Yes, that man who's out of his mind, speaking with strange voices, like demons have taken him over. What's he shouting about now?'

Everyone turned to listen.

'Jesus of Nazareth? What do you want with us? Come to destroy us? I know who you are – the Holy One of God!'

'Quiet!' replied Jesus – and the man was quiet. 'Come out of him!'

The man fell on the ground, peace and healing washing through him.

Everyone gasped – one startled intake of breath. Then the whispering started. 'Did you see that? This teaching is really something – with power over evil!'

And so the word began to spread – like ripples from a stone dropped in the lake – until everyone along the shores of the Sea of Galilee had heard what had happened.

At Simon the Fisherman's Home

Luke 4:38–40

Jesus walked to Simon's home with him after the service was over.

'My mother-in-law is unwell,' said Simon. When they got there, they found her drifting in and out of wakefulness, burnt up with fever. She was too weak even to raise her head.

'Can you help her, please? Is there anything you can do?' Simon asked Jesus.

Jesus bent over her, and spoke out. 'Fever, leave this woman alone! Be gone!'

They watched as the flush ebbed from her face and she sat up, her strength returning.

'Oh, my!' she said, getting out of bed. 'A guest in the house and no food prepared! Sit down, sir, I'll get something good!'

That evening, as the sabbath ended, many came to Jesus for healing. And he healed them all.

What a Catch!

Luke 5:1–11

Jesus' first disciples were four men who fished the waters of the Sea of Galilee from sturdy wooden sailing boats.

ONE DAY, Jesus was standing by the edge of the lake, teaching an ever-growing crowd. Seeing one of Simon's boats, he climbed in, and Simon and his crew pushed off into the shallow waters near the shore. And from the boat Jesus taught the crowd, telling them the good news of the kingdom of God – how to live God's way.

When the crowds had gone, he turned to Simon and said, 'Push out into deep water and let down those nets for a catch!'

'Master!' his friend said with a smile. 'We slaved all night and didn't even catch a sardine. But for you… anything!'

No sooner had the nets floated down through the waves than they were filled with flapping, shining fish. The men heaved, but, as the nets came up, there were ominous tearing sounds.

'Give us a hand!' Simon bellowed across to his other boat, and together they landed the catch – swamping both decks with wriggling, rainbow-scaled beauties. The boats were so low in the water that they had to row back to shore very tentatively, to keep from sinking.

Simon and his friends, James and John, couldn't believe it. Simon fell to his knees among the fish.

'Master!' he said. 'I'm a sinful man, full of faults. You'd better go – you're too good for me.'

'Don't be afraid!' Jesus said with a smile. 'I'm not leaving. You come with me, and we'll fish for people instead!'

And the fishermen left their boats on the shore and set off with Jesus. The adventure was just beginning.

A New Way to Live

MATTHEW 5, 6

JESUS SAW THAT GREAT crowds were following him, and so he went up on a mountainside and sat down. Those who wanted to learn drew close, and he taught them many things.

'Our Law tells you what to do, and what not to do. That's good – I haven't come to change it one bit. But I want to take things a bit deeper.

'You know the Law says, "An eye for an eye, and a tooth for a tooth", but this is what I say: Don't fight back. If someone hits you on one cheek, turn the other.

'You have heard, "Love your neighbour and hate your enemy", but I say: Love your enemy, and pray for those who hurt you. It's how God treats you. God sends sunshine to all – good and bad alike, blessing everyone.

'It's so easy to find faults. Don't do it — unless you want to be judged by the same standards. Why look at the speck of sawdust in your brother's eye, when there's a great plank in your own? Sort out your own life, and then you might be able to help someone else.

'And don't spend all your time filling your cupboards. Things are so fragile. They get old and tatty, or stolen. Store up real treasure in heaven — where it'll never get old, and there are no thieves! Whatever you value, that's what you give your life to.

'So don't worry about what to eat or what clothes to wear. Life is more than mealtimes, and clothes don't define you. Look at those birds. Have you ever seen them storing the harvest? No! But God is feeding them. And these wild flowers — have you seen fabric as beautiful as that? If God dresses this hillside with such care, don't you think he'll look after you, too?

'Put the kingdom of God first, and God won't let you down.'

This collection of Jesus' teachings in Matthew's Gospel is often called the Sermon on the Mount.

How to Pray

MATTHEW 6:5–15,
7:7–11

JESUS LOOKED AT the people sitting on the mountainside, listening to his words, and he wanted to tell them more about the ways of God. Above all, he wanted them to know how to pray.

'When you need something,' Jesus continued, 'ask God for it, and it will be given to you. Look for it, and you will find it. Go knocking at the door, and you will be welcomed in. When children ask their father for bread, does their father give them a stone? Of course not! Or if they want fish, would he put a snake on their plates? So don't hesitate to ask God, who wants to answer with good gifts.

'Prayer has nothing to do with showing off. If you go somewhere public to pray, and make sure everyone is listening, then you've already had what you were after. This is how you should do it. Go into your room and close the door, and pray simply to your Father. You don't have to use fancy language, or go on and on trying to convince God. After all, God knows you inside out, and wants what's best for you. Pray like this, instead:

The prayer Jesus taught is sometimes called the Lord's Prayer and sometimes the Our Father.

'Our Father in heaven,
hallowed be your name,
your kingdom come,
your will be done
on earth as in heaven.
Give us today our daily bread.
Forgive us our sins
as we forgive those who sin against us.
Lead us not into temptation
but deliver us from evil.

'For if you forgive people for the hurt they have done to you, then you will receive forgiveness from God for the things you have done to others.'

31

The Two House Builders

MATTHEW
7:24–27

In the land where Jesus lived, heavy rainstorms after a season of dry weather can cause sudden floods.

JESUS HAD TAUGHT the people many things on the mountainside, and he searched their faces thoughtfully. Would they have the courage to live by his teaching?

'These words of mine should be put into practice,' he said, 'and if they are, they'll give your life a good, solid basis. Like this.

'A man was out looking for somewhere to build his home. He came to some good solid rock. "This is the spot!" he said, and set to work. It was hard preparing the ground, but he knew it would be worth it. He was just smoothing the roof flat when he felt the wind change, and looked up to see a mass of black clouds above him. He scurried inside as the downpour began. He heard the water pounding the roof and rushing over the hard mud walls. The man could hear another sound, too, a mighty whoosh of water. He peeped through the door and saw the river rising fast – a flash flood. But he was out of its reach, and his house stayed firm.

'But those who hear my words, and don't put them into practice, are like this. A foolish man looked for a good place to build a house. Down by the river was a sandy spot. "This'll be easy digging!" said the man.

In no time at all he had thrown up a house, and was sitting
inside when the storm blew up. He heard the rain pounding on
the roof, and soon it was dripping through. He noticed that his
feet were getting damp. Then, his pots and baskets began to
float about. He peeped outside. "Help!" he cried, as he saw the
brown flood waters surging up his path. 'I'd better get out
quickly!' Just then, the house groaned its last, and
with an almighty crash – splash! – it crumbled
into the flood.'

33

Water into Wine

JOHN 2:1–11

CANA, NEAR NAZARETH, was alight with joy and ringing to the sounds of singing and dancing. For a wedding was taking place, and many guests had come, including Jesus with his new disciples. His mother Mary was also there.

But, as day faded into evening, Mary noticed something. The servants were anxious, scurrying from one container of wine to another. She went up to Jesus and said, 'They've run out of wine.'

'Mother – why are you telling me this? It isn't my time yet.'

But Mary simply went to the servants and said, 'Do whatever he tells you.'

Propped up against the wall were six huge stone water jars, each of which could hold about one hundred litres. They were not for storing drinking water, but for water used to purify and cleanse according to Jewish religious laws. Jesus went over to the servants.

'Fill those jars with water.' So they did, with jugful after jugful, until the empty jars brimmed over with fresh, clear water.

'Now, draw some off and take it to the master of ceremonies.' The servants looked at one another uneasily, but did as he said.

The master of ceremonies took a sip, swilled it around his mouth, and swallowed. A broad smile spread across his face. It was wine — full-bodied, rich and warm. He called the bridegroom over, not knowing where the wine had come from.

'People usually bring out the finest wines first – and then serve up the cheap stuff when people have already had a few. But not you! You've saved the best vintage till now!'

And so, on the third day of his ministry, Jesus revealed his glory. He turned water into wine as a sign – pointing the way to the riches of God's kingdom. And the disciples put their faith in him.

The host at a wedding was expected to provide wine in abundance for all the guests. According to John, turning water into wine was Jesus' first miracle.

Jesus and Nicodemus

JOHN 3:1–21

NICODEMUS, THE SCHOLAR and member of the Jewish ruling council, came to see Jesus quietly at night.

'Rabbi, we all know you are from God. No one could point the way to God with miracles as you do unless God himself were behind it.'

Jesus' reply stretched Nicodemus' understanding.

'Yes, and I tell you the truth. No one can see what I'm pointing to – that is, God's kingdom – unless he is born again as a child of God.'

'How can a man be born when he is old?' asked Nicodemus. 'He can hardly go back to his mother's womb and begin again!'

'Listen – I'm telling you the truth. To see the kingdom of God you need a different type of birth – a birth of water and spirit. The body gives birth to a body, but it takes the Spirit to give birth to spirit.'

Nicodemus sat back.

'Why are you so surprised?' Jesus asked. 'Don't you understand that you must be born again? Think of the wind hovering, blowing where it pleases over the earth. You can hear its sound, but who knows where it comes from and where it's going? It is like this with those born of the Spirit. Their sails are filled by the wind of God.'

'What do you mean?'

'Your job is to teach. You of all people need to know the truth. And this is the truth:

Nicodemus was a member of a religious group called the Pharisees. They were committed to understanding and obeying the laws in the Jewish scriptures.

'God so loved the world that he sent his one and only Son, so that everyone who believes will not die, but be given the gift of eternal life. God sent his Son to rescue the world, not to condemn it! Light has come into the world, but some prefer to lurk in the shadows. Yet the light is there, shining brightly, for all who live by the truth.'

And so Nicodemus left, his mind a buzz of new ideas, and his heart opening to the light.

The Man Through the Roof

MARK 2:1–12

'HAVE YOU HEARD?' said one to another. 'Jesus is back here in Capernaum – full of God's power – and he's even healing the sick!'

'What are we waiting for? Let's go!' came the reply. But there was one man who could only watch the running crowds. He did not join them, because he couldn't walk. He was paralysed.

However, this man had good friends. 'We're taking you on a little trip!' they said, picking up the mat he was lying on, and carrying him through the crowds.

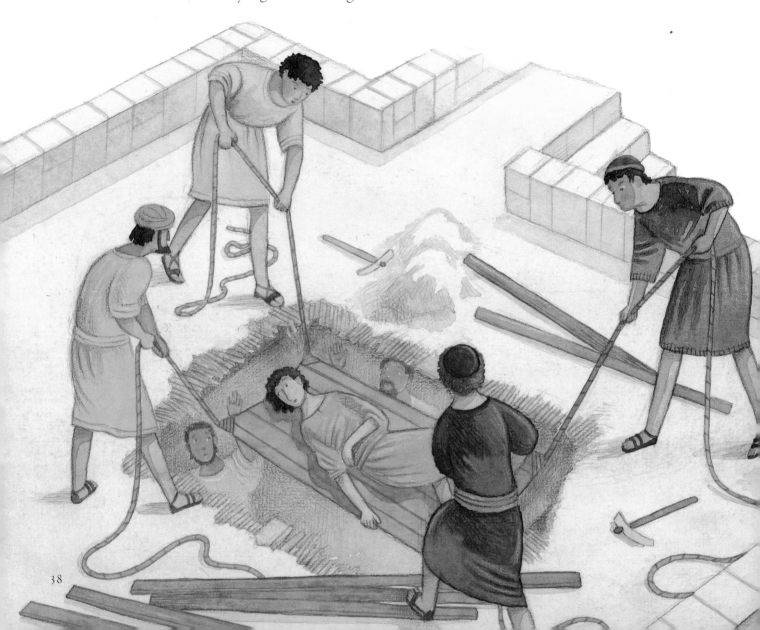

'Excuse me please, can we get through?'

'You'll have to wait your turn.'

They waited, and waited, but still could not get through. So at last they made their way up onto the roof, and began to dig their way down.

Inside, religious leaders were watching Jesus carefully when they became aware of a trickle of dust from the ceiling. Soon, great chunks of rubble came tumbling down and dust billowed around them, making them cough and splutter. Faces appeared at the hole.

'Sorry about that!' the friends said, as they began to lower the paralysed man down on ropes. But Jesus looked up and smiled. What faith they had!

Jesus turned to the rather grimy man on the mat and said, 'Friend, your sins are forgiven.'

The religious teachers gasped. 'Who is he, anyway, saying he can forgive sins? Only God can do that! He's speaking a terrible blasphemy – claiming he's God!'

'Which do you think is easier: to say "Your sins are forgiven", or "Get up and walk"? To prove to you that the Son of Man has the authority to forgive...' and he turned to the man on the mat, '... get up, pick up that mat and go home!'

And that is what the man did – he grabbed his mat and hopped through the crowd, praising God.

The story spread among the people. 'We have never seen anything like this before!' they said.

The Sower and the Seed

Matthew
13:1–23

IT WAS A PERFECT SPRING DAY. The sky was shining blue, the ground was warming in the sun, and the air was full of birdsong. Jesus stood on the shores of the Sea of Galilee, hemmed in by an ever-growing crowd. They were so eager to hear him speak that they hardly left him room to breathe. So he got into a boat and pushed off, coming to a stop a little way from the shore.

Then, as the sunlight danced on the water, and the waves lapped the boat gently, Jesus looked up, and saw a man in the fields behind the crowds. He was taking handfuls of seed from his bag, and throwing them in high golden arcs as he walked. Jesus smiled.

'Listen to this!' he began. 'Once, a farmer went out to sow his seeds. But some fell on the hard path, and were gobbled up by birds as soon as they touched the ground. Some fell among the rocks, where the soil was thin and poor. Before long, the first green shoots sprang up. They looked promising. But then, the sun rose high in the sky, baking everything in its scorching heat. The green soon faded to brown, and the plants withered and died. They had no roots to sustain them. Other seeds fell among the thorns, which grew faster than the delicate shoots of wheat, choking them and blocking out their light, so that they could not bear any grain. But there were some seeds that fell on good soil, which sent down strong roots, and grew up to the light. In time, the wheat ripened in the sun, and when the farmer returned to harvest it,

Sowing grain was traditionally done by scattering handfuls of seed onto a ploughed field. This is sometimes called broadcast sowing.

he found that these seeds had multiplied thirty, sixty or even a hundred times!'

Jesus paused a moment, looking at the faces turned to him. 'He who has ears to hear, let him hear!'

When the crowds had gone, and they were by themselves, the twelve disciples, and the other followers, asked Jesus about the stories he told.

'Don't you understand this parable? Don't you understand any of them? This is what it means.

'The farmer is sowing the word of God. Some people are like seeds that fall on the path. No sooner do they fall than they are snatched away – they will never grow. Others are like the seeds that fall on rocky places. They hear the word, and are full of enthusiasm, beginning to grow. But at the first hint of trouble or difficulty, they wither up inside, and quickly fall away. Others are like the seeds that fall among thorns. They hear and respond, but then all the crush of everyday concerns, and the love of money, crowd in on them, and the word never bears fruit in their lives. But others, like the seeds on good soil, hear the word, accept it, and live lives full of abundance. They bear fruit thirty, sixty or even a hundred times what was sown.'

Parables of the Kingdom

MATTHEW
13:31–32,
34–35, 44–46

JESUS SAT IN THE BOAT which bobbed on the Sea of Galilee, telling story after story to the crowds who lined the shore.

'The kingdom of heaven is like a tiny mustard seed. A farmer once took one carefully from the palm of his hand. It was so small that his hard-working fingers could hardly feel it. Then he bent down and planted it. As time passed, he watched with joy as it grew and spread to become such a large plant! And his face broke into a smile when he saw the birds of the air come to find shelter among its branches.'

Jesus unwrapped the secrets of the kingdom of God for the people, by telling stories, or parables, like these – just as the poet wrote in the book of Psalms so many years before:

*'I will open my mouth
in parables,
and speak of things
that have been hidden away
since the creation of the world.'*

A parable is a story which has a deeper meaning.

He told them more.

'The kingdom of heaven is like an old wooden treasure chest. One day, a man was walking across a field when he stumbled on something. He stopped, and set to work digging it up. He scraped away the dirt, fiddled with the catch, and when it burst open, he could hardly believe his eyes! Quickly, he reburied the chest, went away, and sold his own land. Then, he bought the field from the farmer with joy in his heart and a spring in his step. The treasure was now his by right.

'Or look at it this way. The kingdom of heaven is like a merchant searching faraway markets for pearls. One day, he found one of such purity, such beauty, that it took his breath away. He knew he had found the once in a lifetime, one in a million, pearl of great price. So he sold everything he had gladly, and bought it.'

43

Jesus Calms the Storm

Mark 4:35–41

Dangerous storms still funnel down from the hills to the Sea of Galilee.

IT HAD BEEN A DAY FOR STORYTELLING, on which Jesus had told many parables of God's kingdom to the eager crowds who stood along the shore. But now, the sun had slipped down in the sky, and the clouds glowed red above the hills.

'That's enough for today!' he said to the disciples. 'Let's cross to the other side of the lake.'

Andrew and the others got the boat ready – pulling up the anchor and making ready the sails – and steered it out into the lapping waves. Jesus settled down in the back of the boat. He was soon soothed to sleep by the gentle wash of water under him. Other boats joined them.

Suddenly, without warning, the wind rushed down from the hills like a pack of hungry wolves – snarling and snapping at the sails, whipping the water into a boiling, angry roar. Waves barged into the side of the boat, knocking the disciples off their feet.

'Quick! Pull the ropes!' ordered Andrew.

'Turn her round to shore!' bellowed Simon Peter.

But it was no use: they were taking in water fast. They were buffeted, helpless, sinking.

'Is he still asleep?' called Matthew, looking at Jesus.

'He's lying on a cushion – soaked through! How can he still be asleep at a time like this?'

'Wake up!' they shouted through the salt spray. 'Teacher, we're all going to drown! Don't you care?'

Jesus got up, and looked at the dripping, terrified men, the howling wind, and the towering waves. He called out in a loud voice, 'Quiet! Be still!'

The wind lowered its head with a whimper, and the sea smoothed to a glittering sheen.

Then he turned to the disciples. 'Why so scared? Don't you have faith in me?'

But a different fear gripped them now.

'Who is this man? The wind and the waves obey him as if he were their master!'

Jairus' Daughter

MARK 5:21–43

JAIRUS SAT AT HIS DAUGHTER'S BEDSIDE, holding her limp hand. He looked at her face – she was so pale, so still. 'She's only twelve – too young to be dying!' he murmured. He stood up and walked over to the window, craning his neck as he looked out.

'Can you see anything yet?' he called up to the flat roof, where a servant was keeping watch.

'Yes! A sail! I think it's them – and you should see the crowds on the shore!' At last Jesus and his disciples were on their way back from the other side of the lake, after the extraordinary storm the night before.

But now there was no time to lose. Jairus ran down to the quayside to fetch Jesus, but the whole town seemed to have got there before him. They all knew Jairus, the respected leader of the synagogue, their place of worship, and had heard how ill his only daughter was. So they stood back, and let him through. When Jairus reached Jesus, he fell at his feet.

'My daughter is dying. Please come, and lay your hands on her, so she will live!'

Jesus gently raised him to his feet, and began to walk alongside him towards his home.

Where Jesus went, the crowds followed. They jostled and pressed on every side, slowing Jesus and Jairus down at times. Suddenly, Jesus stopped. He turned to the crowd.

'Who touched my clothes?' he asked. He had felt power flowing from him.

The disciples were surprised. 'What do you

mean, "Who touched my clothes?" Can't you see the crowds? Everyone's touched your clothes!'

But Jesus just waited, looking at the faces in front of him.

Slowly, with her head hanging low, a woman took one step forwards, and sank to her knees. 'I meant no harm – I never thought anyone would notice! I've been bleeding for twelve years,' she told him. 'I've spent every penny on doctors who only made matters worse. I thought, if I could just touch your clothes, I would be well… And it's true, isn't it?' she said. 'I'm healed!'

'Daughter, you stepped out in faith, and now you are healed. Go, and live a life of peace – free from pain.'

Even as Jesus was speaking, a solemn group came from Jairus' house, and spoke to Jairus softly. 'Come now, come home and leave the teacher in peace. It's too late for your daughter. She's dead.'

'Don't be afraid,' cut in Jesus. 'Just believe.'

And he walked steadily on, with Jairus at his side. They arrived to find the house echoing with crying and wailing, taken over by black-draped mourners.

'Why all the tears and howling? She's only asleep, not dead!' Jesus said.

'What do *you* know?' the mourners sneered, and continued their lamenting. Jesus wasted no time. He threw them out of the house, and took the girl's mother and father, and the disciples who were with him. They went into the room where she was lying. He sat down at her side, and took her cold, white hand.

'*Talitha koum,*' he said, which means, 'Little girl, get up!'

And that was what she did – she got up and started walking around! For a moment, everyone stood there awestruck, astonished, open-mouthed with amazement. Then the house burst into glorious life – ringing with shouts of joy and laughter, and tears of thankfulness.

'She'll be hungry,' said Jesus. 'Better get her something to eat!'

And he told those present not to speak of what had happened in that room to anyone.

The Bread of Life

JOHN 6:1–14, 25–35

JESUS CROSSED THE SEA OF GALILEE by boat, heading for the quiet mountains on the other side. But the crowds came after him, running along the shore, for they had seen him heal the sick.

Jesus sat down on the mountainside, and watched the crowds gathering. It was nearing the time of the Passover feast, when the Jews remember how Moses led them from slavery and through the wilderness.

'The crowds will be hungry,' Jesus said to Philip. 'Where can we buy food?'

Philip was startled. 'Even a whole heap of silver would buy less than a mouthful each!'

Andrew added, 'Here is a boy with five barley loaves and two small fish. Hardly a feast!'

'Tell them all to sit down,' Jesus said.

With a ripple and a murmur they sat on the soft green grass. The disciples ran their eyes over the crowd – probably about five thousand men.

The boy gave his bundle of food to Jesus, biting his lip, and sat down at his feet.

Jesus gave thanks for the bread, and broke it. But the more he broke, the more was left. It seemed to grow in his hands, like rising dough – there was more and more every time he broke it. He shared the mounds of broken bread with the boy and the crowds, and then he did the same with the fish. And as five thousand people ate their fill, quietened

50

by awe, they remembered how Moses had fed the people in the
wilderness.

'Collect up all the leftovers!' Jesus said to the twelve, and each
one gathered a basketful.

Later, Jesus explained this miracle, this sign that pointed to
God. 'Don't work for food that won't last, but for food that
will feed your spirit for ever.

'I am the bread of life, the living bread,' he said. 'If anyone
comes to me, they will never go hungry again.'

*This miracle with
the loaves and fishes
is often called the
feeding of the
five thousand.*

Who is Jesus?

MATTHEW 16:1–3,
13–28

*The disciple called
Simon Peter said
that Jesus was the
Messiah. This word
comes from the
Hebrew and means
'chosen king'. From
the Greek is another
word with the same
meaning: Christ.*

SOME RELIGIOUS LEADERS came to Jesus and questioned him.
They wanted him to say who he really was – and to prove it
with a sign, or a miracle.

'You look at the clouds in the sky,' he answered, 'and say, "It's
going to be stormy – the sky is red this morning." You've
learned to read the weather, but you can't read the signs of the
times – the signs you are given.'

Later, when the disciples had settled down for the evening at a
town called Caesarea Philippi, Jesus asked, 'What are people
saying about me? Who do they think I am?'

They replied, 'Some say you are John the Baptist; others say
Elijah, Jeremiah or one of the other prophets, returned from
long ago.'

'But what about you?' Jesus' eyes searched their fire-lit faces.
'Who do you say I am?'

For a while, there was silence. Then Simon Peter spoke. 'You
are the Christ, the Messiah, Son of the Living God.'

'God bless you, Simon. This answer came to you straight
from my Father in heaven. No one told you.' Jesus paused,
thoughtful. 'This answer is going to be the bedrock of my
church – the people who follow me – and in honour of it I'm
going to call you Peter, "The Rock".

'This church will be so powerful that the gates of hell itself
will not defeat it. And I will give you the keys to the kingdom
of heaven – nothing will be closed off from you. Whatever you
bind on earth will be bound in heaven.'

But he warned them not to tell anyone that he was the Christ,
God's chosen one.

However, there was a darker side to this good news.

It was time for Jesus to turn to face Jerusalem, and all that he must suffer there. He tried to prepare his disciples, but they could not yet understand.

Shining with Light

MATTHEW
17:1–13

JESUS TOOK PETER AND THE brothers James and John, and
together they climbed a high mountain. There, far from the
crowds, they watched as Jesus was transformed before their eyes.
His face shone like the bright Middle Eastern sun – pure and
dazzling – and his clothes were as white as light itself. And as
he stood, light pouring from him, he was joined by Moses, the
Lawgiver, and Elijah, the great prophet. The three of them
talked deeply together, far above the everyday world.

Peter's face was full of wonder – he wanted to watch them for
ever! 'Lord!' he said. 'It is so good to be here, right now. Shall I
build shelters for you, Moses and Elijah?'

But the words were not out of his mouth when a shining
cloud of glory came over them, and they were all enveloped in
its bright, luminous mist. Then a voice came from the heart of
the cloud:

'This is my Son, the one I love, my pride and joy. Listen to him!'

At the sound of that voice, Peter, James and John were gripped with terror, and fell face down onto the ground. But Jesus came and touched them gently. 'Come, don't be afraid. Get up!'

And as they raised their eyes, they saw only Jesus.

Down the mountain they came, over the rocks and streams, talking about what they had seen.

'Not a word of this to anyone, not until the Son of Man has been raised from the dead,' urged Jesus.

And after that, the three disciples had no doubt as to who Jesus really was.

The story of Jesus appearing to his disciples in a heavenly light is often called the Transfiguration. Some people think it took place on Mount Hermon.

Forgiveness

MATTHEW
18:21–35

*This parable of the
unmerciful servant
is a reminder to
Christians to
forgive even those
who have done
great wrong.*

PETER CAME TO JESUS WITH A QUESTION.

'Lord, how many times should I forgive someone? Seven?'

'You aren't even close, Peter! Not seven, more like seventy-seven! Listen to this story:

'The kingdom of heaven is like a king who was busy straightening out his accounts, checking who owed him money. One of his servants was brought before him. He had borrowed a fortune – sacks and sacks of gold.

' "Well, pay up!" bellowed the king. But how could the servant pay him back? The debt was vast.

' "I can't!" muttered the terrified servant.

' "Then it's the slave market for you! I'll sell you, your wife and your children, not to mention all your belongings."

' "Please, give me more time! I promise I'll pay, but it may take me a while.'

'The king looked at the miserable figure on his knees before him, and his heart softened.

' "Very well, I cancel your debt. Off you go before I change my mind!"

'As the servant left the king's chamber, he grabbed one of the other servants by the neck.

' "You owe me a few coins! Pay up

now!" His hands closed around the man's throat.

' "Please, give me more time! I promise I'll pay!" the man gasped.

'Did he let him off? No! He dragged him to prison, and wouldn't allow him out until he'd paid.

'The other servants were appalled. They went to tell the king.

' "How could you be so wicked?" he said. "I cancelled your debt – shouldn't you have done the same? Guards! Take him away, and have him tortured until he pays!"

'And this is how it will be for you, unless you forgive your brother from the heart. Think how much God has to forgive you for. Shouldn't you then forgive one another?'

The Good Samaritan

ON ONE OCCASION, an expert in God's Law stood up and asked Jesus a question.

'Teacher,' he said, as everyone turned to look at him, 'what must I do to inherit eternal life?'

He was keen to pit his wits against Jesus. These 'experts' seemed to like nothing better than a good argument about religion.

'What's written in the books of the Law? I'd like to hear how you understand it,' Jesus replied.

The expert cleared his throat, and recited two verses.

' "Love the Lord your God with all your heart and with all your soul and all your mind," and "Love your neighbour as yourself." '

'A very good answer,' said Jesus. 'If you do all that, you'll have eternal life.' And he looked away, about to start talking to someone else.

'And…' said the expert, feeling a little annoyed – this was hardly the great debate he wanted, '… and who is my neighbour, exactly?'

But Jesus was not going to be drawn into an argument. He signalled to the expert to sit down, looked at him for a moment, and began to tell a story.

'A man was going down from Jerusalem to Jericho. You know the road, and how it passes through rocky hills that are just right for ambush. Well, a gang of robbers was hiding there, keeping a lookout for a likely victim. When they saw this man, they sprang into the

road, shouting and waving great, heavy sticks.
The traveller dropped his things and tried to
run, but he didn't stand a chance. The robbers jumped on him
and beat him to the ground. They stripped off his clothes, took
everything and cleared off – leaving him for dead.

'It was not long before a priest came by, dressed in fine robes.
He saw the figure lying by the side of the road. As he drew
closer, he saw the bruises and the blood. Perhaps he had
important work to do at the Temple, and had to keep himself
clean. Whatever the reason, he skirted around the broken figure,
and walked by on the other side of the road. The wounded man
could hear his footsteps growing fainter, but was too weak to
cry out.

*Priests were in
charge of the
worship at the
Jewish Temple in
Jerusalem. Levites
helped with the
day-to-day running
of the Temple.*

'Then, at last, someone else approached. It was another religious man – a Levite this time. He, too, saw the figure lying by the road, and hesitated. Perhaps he was in a hurry to get to the Temple as well, or perhaps he thought the robbers were still around. Whatever the reason, he sidestepped the broken figure and walked by on the other side. The wounded man would not be able to hold on much longer – lying there under the hot sun, with his mouth full of dust.

'A third figure appeared. A Samaritan…' Jesus paused while a murmur spread through the listeners. Everyone in the crowd felt the same about Samaritans – they were no good!

'A Samaritan,' repeated Jesus, 'saw the man lying by the road, and his heart was filled with pity. He jumped off his donkey and rushed over. Raising the man's head, he gave him water from his own bottle. 'You're safe now,' he said. He washed the wounds, poured on wine and oil to clean and soothe them, and then ripped up his spare clothes to bandage him.

'The man cried out in pain as the Samaritan lifted him onto his donkey, and led him gently to an inn. He ordered a comfortable bed, and patiently fed him and gave him drink. He watched over him all night. Next morning, he spoke to the innkeeper. 'Look after him,' he said, handing over silver coins. 'I will pay you on my way back for any extra you spend on him.'

'Now,' said Jesus, looking at the expert, 'which one of these

The Jews looked down on Samaritans as outsiders. They accused them of not worshipping God in the right way.

three was a neighbour to the man who was robbed?'

The expert hesitated. All his fine arguments, all his cleverness suddenly felt rather empty, rather pointless.

'It was…' – he could not bring himself to say the word Samaritan – '… It was the man who showed him kindness.'

'Go, and do likewise.'

An Invitation to God's Feast

LUKE 14:1–24

JESUS SPENT THE EVENING at the house of an important religious leader. His every word, and every action, was carefully observed. And there was plenty to keep the spies interested: Jesus had healed a man even though it was the sabbath, and had asked his host some very difficult questions.

As the night drew on, and the lamplight flickered, a man looked up from the table and said to Jesus, 'Happy will be the man who eats at the feast God prepares!'

Jesus answered with a story.

'There was once a very rich man who wanted to share his good fortune with his friends.

'"I know!" he said. "I'll throw them all a fabulous feast!" So his servants set to work – buying the finest food and wine, polishing the silver, chopping and stirring. Others went out to deliver the invitations.

'"A feast! How nice!" everyone said.

'The day of the feast came, and the air was heavy with the scent of spices. The rich man sat at the head of a table heaped with fabulous food, drumming his fingers.

'He ordered his servants, "Go and tell the guests it's all ready – we're waiting!" And they scurried off, only to be met by one excuse after another.

'"Is that today? I've just got married, I can't come now!"

'"I've just bought a field – I must go and see to it. Please send my apologies!"

'"Look at these new oxen – five teams of them – aren't they beauties? I'm on my way to see how well they plough my fields. Sorry!"

'The rich man was furious.

'"What?" he roared, thumping the table. "Not one of them coming? Go out into the city streets and alleys, and bring in the hungry and homeless, the injured and the sick!" And they came, hardly believing their luck. But there was still food to spare.

'"Go down the highways, the country lanes, and make the people come. I want my house to be full. Those ungrateful ones, they can stay away!"'

Jesus' parable of the great feast contains a warning that nothing should be more important than accepting the invitation to be part of God's kingdom. Jesus also said that people should come to the kingdom as eagerly as children.

63

The Lost Sheep

LUKE 15:1–7

THE CROWDS WHO GATHERED around Jesus were not all religious people. Tax collectors, who collaborated with the Romans for their own gain, and outcasts – characters from the rougher parts of town – came in droves. They hung on his every word.

The religious leaders – Pharisees and teachers – who had come to hear Jesus drew back in horror when they saw who they were mixing with. 'Just look at the sort of people this man is happy to welcome! He even sits down and eats with them!' So Jesus told them this story.

'Suppose one of you has one hundred sheep. One day, when the sheep are peacefully grazing on the hills, you decide to count them to make sure they are all safe. As you count, you can't help feeling uneasy – there is one sheep you haven't seen lately. Could she be lost?

'Yes, there are only ninety-nine! One is lost! So, you leave the ninety-nine out in the open, and hunt for the lost sheep. You search behind rocks, and in thorn bushes and gullies. You search high and low – not giving up until you find the lost one. And when, at last, you find her, you pick her up and carry her back on your shoulders. Then, you invite all your friends and neighbours round! "Be happy with me! I've found my lost sheep!" And you celebrate long into the night.

'It's just the same with God's kingdom. There is more rejoicing in heaven over one sinner who repents, who stops doing wrong things and turns their life around, than over ninety-nine who don't need to.'

Jesus' parable of the lost sheep is a reminder to Christians that God is on the side of those whose wrongdoing makes them outcasts.

The Good Shepherd

JOHN 10:1–21

ON ANOTHER DAY, Jesus was deep in conversation with the religious leaders. They were familiar with all the holy writings, and had read King David's song, written many years before:

'The Lord is my shepherd...
He makes me lie down in green pastures.'

And so Jesus spoke to them like this:
'If someone climbs into a sheep pen, he's up to no good – he's a sheep stealer. But the man who walks in through the gate is the shepherd. He calls his own sheep by name, and they know his voice, so they'll follow wherever he leads. They stay with him because they know him. If a stranger climbs in and tries to call them out, they simply won't come.' The people listening murmured to each other, wondering what he meant.

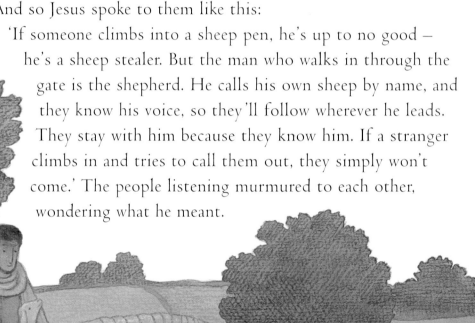

'I am the gate for the sheep. Whoever comes through me will be safe, entering and leaving good, green pastures. A thief comes only to destroy, but I have come to bring life: abundant and overflowing life.

'I am the good shepherd, willing to lay down my life for the sheep. The hired hand doesn't own the sheep – he'll run at the first sign of danger, leaving the flock to be scattered and torn apart by wolves. Not me. I am the good shepherd. I know my sheep, and they know me. And I willingly lay down my life for my sheep.

'And there are other sheep who belong to my flock. They are far away, in other lands. But I will call them. When they hear my voice, they'll come. And there will be just one flock, united under one shepherd.'

Some said, 'The man's mad! Why should we listen to this?'

But others answered, 'No madman ever talked such sense. And no one evil ever restored the sight of the blind.'

The image of a shepherd keeping his sheep within the protective walls of a sheepfold reminds Christians of God's love and care.

The Lost Son

LUKE 15:11–32

This parable is often called the prodigal son: 'prodigal' means spendthrift.

JESUS TOLD THE PEOPLE many stories to show how much God loves those who have lost their way, and how God longs for them to come home to the kingdom of God.

'There was a man who had two sons,' he began. 'The younger said, "Father, give me my share of the inheritance now!" Because the father loved him, he divided his wealth between the two sons then and there.

'The younger son soon packed his bags, and set off travelling. He came to a land far away from his home. There, the gold burned holes in his pockets, and he frittered it away on wild living. But the wild living came to an end when the money ran out, and soon he was desperate. But then things grew even worse, for the shadow of famine darkened that country, and there was hunger everywhere. He was lucky to be hired by a landowner, who set him to work dishing out pigswill on a farm. The younger son's stomach ached with hunger as he fed the pigs. He even became jealous of them, and longed to eat the pods from the swill.

'This shook him up. "All my father's workers have plenty to eat, and I'm starving to death! I'll go back and say: 'Father, I have sinned against heaven and against you. I'm not worthy to be your son, so please, take me on as your servant.'" And he began the long journey home.'

In Jewish Law, pigs are 'unclean' animals, so the young man's job looking after them would have seemed the lowest of the low.

'But his father had been looking out for him, anxiously watching the road. While he was still a long way off, his father saw him trudging through the dust. He saw how thin and ragged his son was, and his heart nearly broke. He ran out to his son, and threw his arms around him while the young man started on his prepared speech.

' "Father, I have sinned against heaven and against you. I'm not worthy to be your son..." But the father was already calling his servants:

' "Quick, get the best robe and put it on him. Put a gold ring on his finger, and some sandals on his bleeding feet. Prepare the prize calf for a feast. We're going to have a party! My son has come back from the dead – come back to life. He was lost, and now I've found him."

'Meanwhile, the older son returned from working in the fields, and heard the singing and dancing.

' "What's going on?"

' "Your brother's back, safe and sound, and there's a feast to celebrate!"

'The older brother was furious, and sulked outside. His father pleaded with him to join them, but the brother's resentment boiled over.

' "I've slaved for you for years – I've never gone against one word you said. And you never even gave me a small goat for my friends. But this son of yours has squandered everything, and you kill the prize calf!"

' "Son! You are always with me. Everything I have is yours. But we have to celebrate. This brother of yours was dead and now he's alive – he was lost and now he's found." '

In this parable, as in the parable of the great feast, the kingdom of heaven is likened to a noisy and joyful party.

The Pharisee and the Tax Collector

LUKE 18:9–14

Jewish men traditionally stood with their hands raised to say their prayers.

JESUS KNEW THERE WERE many people who were sure they were living right with God. They were so confident they were right, they even looked down their noses at everyone else. It was to these people, and especially to the religious leaders, that Jesus now spoke.

'Two men went up to the Temple in Jerusalem to pray. One was a Pharisee, while the other was a tax collector.'

The listeners smiled smugly. They were sure how this one would go. Pharisees were religious experts, on home territory in the Temple.

'The Pharisee stood up and prayed in a loud voice that everyone could hear, "Thank you God, that I am not like all other people – these evil-doers, adulterers and robbers, or even this cheating tax collector here." The tax collector winced. "I go without food twice a week, and give a tenth of my income to the Temple." You could see the Pharisee swell with pride.

'But the tax collector held back, his head bowed low. He would not even look up to heaven. He beat his breast and whispered, "God, have mercy on me, for I am a sinner."

'I tell you, it was the tax collector, and not the Pharisee, who was smiled on by God when he went home. For everyone who tries to show off before God will be brought down, and everyone who is honest before God will be lifted up.'

The words of the tax collector in this parable are known to Christians as the Jesus prayer: 'God, have mercy on me, sinner.'

73

The Little Children and Jesus

MARK 10:13–15

In welcoming children and their mothers, Jesus showed that his message was for ordinary people as they went about their everyday lives.

WHILE JESUS WAS TELLING STORIES to the people, and especially to the religious leaders, the gathering was getting a little noisy. People were bringing their babies and children for Jesus to bless. Little children were running around and playing everywhere, interrupting the serious adult conversation. The disciples tried to hush the children and shoo them away, but Jesus wouldn't hear of it. He spoke sternly to the disciples, and gathered the children to his side. Jesus smiled when he saw their joy, trust and simplicity.

'Let the little children come to me, and don't do anything to stand in their way. For the kingdom of God belongs to little ones such as these. If you don't receive the kingdom like a little child, you won't receive it at all.'

The Rich Young Man

MARK 10:17–31

A RICH YOUNG MAN HAD HUNG BACK, listening intently to Jesus' words. He was sure this teacher had the answers he was looking for. So, as Jesus got up and started to leave, he ran up to him and fell down on his knees in the street.

'Good teacher,' he asked, 'what must I do to inherit eternal life?'

'Why are you calling me good? Only God is good. You know what the Law says: "Do not murder, do not commit adultery, do not steal, do not lie, do not cheat, honour your parents."'

'Teacher!' he replied, dropping the 'good', 'I've kept them all, ever since I was a child.'

The rich young man felt Jesus' eyes searching his heart. He saw the compassion, the understanding, on his face.

'Yes, but there is one thing you still need to do. Go and sell everything you have and give every penny to the poor. Then you will have treasure in heaven.' Jesus took a step forward, stretching out his hand. 'And come, follow me.'

The colour drained from the young man's face and his smile vanished. He got up and walked away with a heavy heart, because he was very wealthy. Jesus shifted his focus to the disciples.

'How hard the rich find it to enter the kingdom of God!' This took the disciples by surprise. 'Yes, hard for those who trust in riches.

It's easier for a camel to go through the eye of a needle than for a rich man to enter the kingdom!'

The disciples murmured among themselves: 'Who then can be saved?'

'For those who trust in themselves, it's impossible. But with God, everything is possible. Many who are first will be last, and the last will be first.'

The Man Born Blind

JOHN 9:1–41

AS JESUS WALKED ALONG THE ROAD, he saw a man who had been blind all his life. His disciples asked, 'Teacher, whose fault is it that this man was born blind? Did he sin, or was it his parents?'

'Sin and blame are nothing to do with it,' replied Jesus. 'This is to do with revealing God's work in his life. As long as it is daylight, we must do God's work. When night comes, it will be too dark. And while I am in the world, I am the light of the world.'

Then he spat on the ground and made mud, which he put on the blind man's eyes. 'Go and wash in the Pool of Siloam,' he said. And the man did so. As he dried his eyes, he saw a red glow through his closed lids.

Then, he opened his eyes wide. And there before him was the sunlight on the pool, and the clear blue sky. He ran straight home to share the news.

Word soon spread among his neighbours.

'Isn't that the blind beggar?'

'No, it can't be!'

'Oh yes it can!' laughed the man, and he told them about Jesus. And they took him to the Pharisees, the religious leaders, who questioned him closely, even calling in his parents as witnesses.

'This Jesus is a sinner!' the Pharisees claimed.

'I don't know if he is a sinner or not. I do know that I was blind, and now I see! How could this man do such a thing if he wasn't from God?'

At this they seized the man, and threw him out of the synagogue.

Jesus came and found him again.

'Do you believe in the Son of Man?' he asked.

'Tell me who he is, and I will!'

'You are looking at him with your own eyes.'

'Lord, I believe!' said the man who had been born blind. And he fell at Jesus' feet and started to worship him.

Christians believe that Jesus' miracles were signs: that he truly had power from God.

79

Lazarus Returns from the Dead

JOHN 11:1–44

MARTHA AND MARY, of Bethany, hurriedly sent the messenger on his way, and turned back to their dear brother, Lazarus. He was slipping away from them, growing weaker and weaker. But they had not given up hope: they were sure Jesus would come and heal him.

Jesus was given the message: 'Lord, your dear friend is ill.'

Jesus said, 'This illness won't end in death, but in God's glory being shown through the Son!' And he waited for two days, beginning to explain what would happen.

'Our friend Lazarus has fallen asleep. I shall go and wake him.'

'But Lord, if he sleeps, he'll recover!' the disciples replied. Jesus had been talking of Lazarus' death, but they did not understand.

When they arrived in Bethany, Lazarus had been buried for four days already, time enough for Martha and Mary's friends to gather together to comfort them. Many had come from Jerusalem, less than three kilometres away.

But Martha kept watch for one person only – and that was Jesus. When she heard he was coming, she rushed out to meet him, while Mary stayed at home. 'Lord!' she cried. 'If you had been here, my brother would not have died! But I know that, even now, God will give you whatever you ask for.'

'Your brother will rise to life,' Jesus answered.

'I know he will, at the resurrection, at the end of time, on the last day.'

'I am the resurrection and the life. The one who believes in me will live, even if they die. Whoever believes in me will never face the empty void of death. Do you believe this?'

'Yes, Lord. I have always believed that you are the Christ, the Son of God, the one God promised would come into this world.' She hung her head, and turned back to the house to fetch Mary.

Martha called her sister to one side and said, 'The teacher is here, asking for you.'

Mary ran out to him, beside herself with grief. She fell down to the ground and said, 'Lord! If you had been here, my brother would not have died!'

Luke's Gospel tells another story about Mary and Martha. In it, Martha gets angry that her sister leaves all the chores to her, but Jesus says that Mary has made the better choice in sitting and listening to his teaching. Nevertheless, in this story about Lazarus, it is Martha who has complete faith in Jesus.

When Jesus saw her sorrow, and saw the tide of pain that was sweeping over everyone there, his heart and spirit were filled with dark distress.

'Where is Lazarus?'

'Come, Lord, and see.'

Jesus wept. Those who were with Mary said, 'Look how much Jesus loved him!'

But others said, 'Why then didn't he come? The one who opened the eyes of the blind could have saved Lazarus!'

Jesus, Martha and Mary came to the tomb in the rock. When Jesus saw it, he wept once more. Then, he stood in front of the cave and said, 'Take away the stone!'

'But Lord, he has been dead four days – the body will smell!' said Martha.

Jesus replied gently, 'Believe, and you will see God's glory.'
So they took away the stone. Jesus looked up and prayed.
'Father, I thank you for listening to me, and I thank you for
always hearing my prayer. Thank you, too, that many will
believe that you sent me because of this.' Then he called out in
a loud voice, 'Lazarus, come out!' And the man who had been
dead came out, with strips of linen wrapped around him, and a
cloth over his face.

Silence swept through those there – the sound of weeping
was no more. Jesus said, 'Take off the grave clothes, and set him
free.'

Zaccheus and the Sycamore Tree

LUKE 19:1–10

Tax collectors such as Zaccheus were disliked. They charged people heavily – some to give as tax to the Romans, and some for themselves.

THERE WAS A BUZZ IN THE Jericho marketplace that morning.

'Jesus is on his way!'

'He's not stopping, though, we'll have to be quick if we want to see him!'

Zaccheus, the chief tax collector, listened carefully. He had heard much of Jesus – he knew Jesus welcomed people others left out. And Zaccheus was often left out, despite his wealth. He had been overcharging taxes, and lining his pockets with the difference – everyone in town knew he had been cheating them.

So he put on his robes, and went out into the street – it was crowded, and Zaccheus was very short.

'Excuse me!' he said, but everyone pretended they hadn't heard. As the crowd grew more excited, he knew Jesus was nearly there. He ran ahead to a quiet place, hitched up his robes and shinned up a tall sycamore tree.

When Jesus, and the crowds, reached the spot, Jesus looked up and saw the well-dressed man through the leaves.

'Zaccheus, come down! I must be your guest for the day.' So Zaccheus scrambled down, and took Jesus home, followed by the astonished crowd. The tax collector could hardly believe what had happened.

He gave orders to his servants – nothing but the best for the Master! But there was a muttering in the crowd:

'Jesus has gone to eat with that cheat! That fraudster!'

Then, Zacchaeus stood up and said, 'Look, Lord! I'm handing over half my possessions to the poor right now, and if I've cheated anyone, I'll go to them and pay them back four times over.'

'What a great day for this house!' Jesus said. 'God's saving love has blessed it! Zacchaeus is also a son of Abraham – a member of the Jewish family. This is what the Son of Man has come to do: to seek and to save what was lost.'

The King on a Donkey

MATTHEW
21:1–11

JESUS AND HIS FOLLOWERS WERE drawing closer to the great city of Jerusalem. When they reached Bethphage, on the Mount of Olives, Jesus turned to two of the disciples.

'Go on ahead,' he said, 'and as soon as you enter the next village you will see a donkey and her colt tied there. Untie them, and bring them to me. If you are challenged, say that the Master needs them, and they will be handed over.' And so the two disciples went ahead, and found the donkey and foal just as Jesus had said. They led them to him, spreading their cloaks over them, and Jesus mounted.

This took place just as Zechariah the prophet had foretold:

'See, your king is coming to you,
humble, riding a donkey,
on a colt, the foal of a donkey.'

The roads were already thronging with crowds gathering for the feast of Passover the following week.

When the people saw Jesus, they drew back to let him pass, bowing down to lay their cloaks on the stony ground. Others ran to the trees, cutting down branches to spread at the donkey's feet.

And all the time, the crowds ahead and the crowds behind accompanied him with their singing and shouting:

'Hosanna to the son of David!'

'Blessed is the one who comes in the name of God!'

'Hosanna in the highest heavens!'

When Jesus entered Jerusalem, the whole city sat up and took notice, buzzing with one question: 'Who is this?'

The crowds pouring through the gates answered, 'This is Jesus, the prophet from Nazareth.'

Matthew's Gospel makes the point that Jesus is the Messiah promised in the ancient Jewish scriptures.

Turning the Tables

MATTHEW
21:12–17

JESUS, RIDING ON A DONKEY, made his way through the streets
of Jerusalem to the Temple, and entered its courtyards. When
he arrived, he found something closer to a market than a place
of worship.

There were stalls where people could change their everyday
money into special 'Temple' money – at a high rate of
commission. Other stalls sold the highly priced doves that
were needed for Temple worship.

Jesus looked at the greedy, haggling stallholders. He saw how worshippers and the poor were being pushed out, and was horrified.

He began overturning the tables, sending the coins clattering over the floor and doves fluttering up between the columns.

He said to them, 'It is written, "My house will be called a house of prayer", but look! You've turned it into a den of thieves.'

Now that the buyers and sellers had been driven out, the blind and the lame came to Jesus at the Temple, and he healed them all. Children, too, filled the courts, running and shouting, 'Hosanna to the son of David!'

'The king has come to save us!'

The chief priests and religious teachers watched as the Temple was changed before their eyes: it was filled with the joy of the healed and the laughter of children. They seethed, spitting with rage.

'Do you hear what these children are calling you?' they demanded.

'Yes!' replied Jesus. 'Have you ever read: "From the lips of children and infants the Lord has called out praises"?'

And after that, he slipped away to spend the night in the peace of nearby Bethany.

Jesus' overturning the tables in the Temple has inspired many Christians to take positive action to overcome injustice.

The Tenants and the Vineyard

MATTHEW
21:23–27, 33–46

Vineyards were built with a watchtower in the corner. so the owner could look out for thieves who might steal the crop!

JESUS RETURNED TO the Temple, and began to speak to the people. But the religious leaders were gathering, and began to question his right to heal and teach. Jesus answered them with a story.

'Once, there was a man who planted a vineyard. He prepared the soil, and planted the young vines in rows stretching across the hillside. He dug a deep pit for the winepress, and built a tall watchtower. And he tended the young shoots as they began to grow.

'But then, he had to take a trip away, so he chose some farmers to be his tenants. When harvest time came, he sent back a servant to collect his profits. But the tenant farmers grabbed him and beat him up, sending him packing without a single grape to show for it.

'So the owner sent another servant, who was struck on the head for his trouble, and thrown out. He sent a third servant, who was killed. This went on and on, and the tenant farmers never paid their rent – instead they either beat or killed every messenger.

'That left just one person – the son he

loved. The owner sent him last of all, saying, "Surely they will respect my son!"

'But no. Instead, they plotted together greedily. "Let's kill him – he's the heir, after all – and then we'll get the inheritance for ourselves!" And that's what they did. They killed him, and threw his body out of the vineyard.

'And what do you think the owner will do then – let them keep the vineyard? No! He will come, full of rage and grief, and kill those tenants, passing the vineyard over to others.'

This story was against the religious leaders, and they knew it. They tried to find a way of arresting Jesus, but they kept a wary eye on the crowd who loved him, and decided to bide their time.

Jesus Anointed

MATTHEW
26:6–16

*John's Gospel says
that the woman who
anointed Jesus was
Mary, the sister
of Martha and
Lazarus.*

JESUS WAS AT THE HOME OF SIMON, in Bethany, sharing a meal with his friends, when a woman came up quietly behind him. In her hands she held an alabaster jar, full of perfume made of a precious ointment called nard. She raised the jar up, broke it, and poured the perfume over his head.

There was a gasp at this reckless generosity: 'What a waste!' the guests blustered indignantly. 'That perfume was worth a year's wages! It could have been sold, and the money given to the needy.' The woman trembled under the torrent of harsh words raining down on her.

But Jesus silenced them: 'Leave her alone. Why are you giving her grief over this? She has done a beautiful thing for me – given to me without holding back. If you are so eager to help the poor, you can do that any time you like – there are enough days and enough poor. But you will not always have me, and so she did what she could for me now. She has anointed my body for burial – preparing me for my death.

'Wherever the Gospel story is told, so will be the story of her abundant love!'

It was at this point that Judas Iscariot, one of Jesus' chosen
companions, slipped away through the darkness, making his
way to the chief priests. The religious leaders were whispering
together, looking for some sly way to have Jesus arrested and
killed – 'but not during the Passover, or we could have a
riot on our hands!' They could hardly believe their
luck when Judas stepped into the dim
lamplight, and offered to betray him into
their grasp. They promised to give him
silver coins, and from that night on
Judas began to watch for the right
moment to betray his Master.

Jesus Washes His Disciples' Feet

JOHN 13:1–35

To this day, Christians still reenact the ceremony of footwashing as a sign of their willingness to serve one another.

IT WAS JUST BEFORE THE Passover feast, and Jesus knew that the time had come for him to leave the world, and go back to his heavenly Father. He had loved his own people since the beginning. Now he would stretch out his arms, and show them how much.

Jesus knew he had come from God, and was going home to God, and so he stood up from the table where the meal was spread out and wrapped a towel round his waist. Pouring water into a bowl, he knelt down and began to wash his disciples' feet.

'Lord!' gasped Simon Peter. 'Are *you* going to wash *my* feet?'

'You don't understand now, but you will in time,' replied Jesus.

'I can't let you do that, not ever!'

'Unless I wash you, you can't be part of me.'

'Then wash not just my feet, but my head and hands too!'

Jesus returned to the Passover table.

'Do you understand? I'm your teacher, your Lord, and yet this is how I teach and rule, giving you an example to follow. Serve each other humbly, washing one another's feet.

'Now that you know how to live, be blessed by doing it.'

Then, Jesus' eyes filled with shadows as he looked around the table.

'One of you is going to betray me! I tell you the truth. As it says in the psalms,

> ' "Even my close friend, one I trusted,
> who shares my bread,
> will turn against me." '

'Who, Lord?' asked John. Jesus dipped bread in the dish, and gave it to Judas.

'Whatever you are going to do, do quickly.' Judas took the bread, and left. It was night.

'My children, I only have a short time left with you,' Jesus said. 'So I give you a new command: love one another, just as I have loved you. And love will always be your badge of belonging – the sign that you are mine.'

The Last Supper

MARK 14:12–26

THE PASSOVER FESTIVAL HAD BEGUN, and the people of Jerusalem were gathering together. At the feast, a lamb was eaten to remember how God had saved their people in the time of Moses. In those days, the sacrifice of a lamb had protected them as the shadow of death passed over the land.

As darkness fell, Jesus and his friends began to share the feast of Passover together. They ate the roast lamb, bitter herbs and flat bread in the flickering light, telling the story of how their ancestors had been rescued from Egypt, and how Moses had lead them to freedom.

And as they shared their last meal together, Jesus took some bread, gave thanks to God, and broke it in his hands. He gave it to his disciples, saying, 'Take it; this is my body.'

Then, he took a cup of wine, gave thanks and offered it to them. They all drank from the cup. 'This is my blood of the covenant – the promise of God – which is poured out for many.'

Jesus knew that the time had come for him to be betrayed. As the Passover feast ended, he looked at his closest friends. Judas, who had shared his bread, had already slipped away into the night. The others were full of sadness, for Jesus had spoken of leaving them. They finished the meal with a hymn, left the safety of the upstairs room where they had shared Passover, and set off into the shadows for the Mount of Olives nearby.

Christians repeat Jesus' words and actions from the Last Supper in their most important ceremony, often called Holy Communion.

Only Darkness

MARK 14:27–42

JESUS, AND THE ELEVEN, walked through dark and shadowed streets towards the Mount of Olives.

'You will all fall away,' Jesus told them. 'Like sheep whose shepherd has been struck down, you will scatter.'

Peter burst out, 'Whatever the others do, I will never leave you!'

But Jesus insisted. 'Tonight, before the cock crows twice, you will deny you know me three times.'

'Even if I have to die with you, I will never deny you!' Peter protested.

'Never, Lord!' they all said.

They came to the Garden of Gethsemane, where, in the olive grove, Jesus asked them to wait while he prayed. He took Peter, James and John with him. In the spaces between the olive trees they could see nothing, only darkness.

'My sorrow is a heavy load – it is crushing me,' Jesus said. 'Crushing me down into the pit – the darkest grave. Will you stay close, and keep watch for me?' Jesus stepped a little further into the night, and fell trembling to the ground.

'My dear Father, nothing is impossible with you. Take this cup of pain from me,' he prayed. The prayer continued through the dark hours, as desert foxes padded closer to the city, and as the birds hid among the leaves. 'Yet not my will, but yours be done.' He went back to his friends.

'Simon, are you asleep? Could you not even stay awake for an hour –

98

for me?' Again Jesus went, and again he prayed. When he returned, his friends were once more heavy-eyed with sleep, and did not know what to say to him.

For a third time he went and prayed, and a third time he returned.

'Still sleeping? Get up! The hour has come. Look, my betrayer is here!'

A Friend Who Betrayed

MARK 14:43–50,
53–54, 66–72

IN THE GARDEN OF GETHSEMANE, Judas, one of the twelve disciples, stepped out of the shadows. Behind him was a mob armed with swords and clubs, there at the orders of the priests and teachers, and elders of the faith.

'Rabbi – teacher!' Judas said, and greeted him with a kiss. It was the sign the mob was waiting for, and they seized Jesus.

'Am I so like the leader of a revolution, then, that you must come for me with drawn swords? I have been with you every day in the Temple, and you did not arrest me there. But what must be, must be.' At this, all those who had been with him fled through the olive trees.

But Peter hesitated, and turned to watch the mob leading Jesus away. He followed, at a distance. When they reached the High Priest's house, Peter slipped into the courtyard after them. There, some of the High Priest's guards stopped by the fire. Peter stopped with them, stretching out his numbed fingers in the orange glow, listening for any hint of what was happening to Jesus.

Just then, a servant girl walked by. She paused, and stared at Peter.

'You were with that man, Jesus from Nazareth, weren't you?' she asked.

'What are you talking about?' Peter bluffed, and moved away from the firelight as the sound of the first cockcrow rang in his ears.

'Yes, he was, wasn't he?' she asked the others.

'No!' Peter said.

After a while, they asked him themselves, 'Surely you were with him. Anyone can tell you're from Galilee!' Then, Peter began to curse and swear, terrified.

'I tell you I don't know the man!'

But then, as the darkness of night faded to grey, he heard the cock crow a second time. He remembered Jesus' words: 'Before the cock crows twice, you will deny you know me three times.' And Peter was stricken with remorse, and began to weep.

A Crooked Trial

MARK 14:53–65

A proper trial should have been held during the hours of daylight; but Jesus' trial was part of an unjust conspiracy.

AS PETER WARMED HIS HANDS in the High Priest's courtyard, questioned by a servant girl, Jesus was brought before the leaders of the Temple who had been summoned together that night. They were sure Jesus' teaching was dangerous. He and his followers would bring them a great deal of trouble, and it was better to put an end to it now, they reasoned. They tried to find evidence against him so they could have him put to death. But they could find none. They called many witnesses, who served up a pack of lies about him, but they all told a different story. And, as lies and accusations beat down on him, Jesus stood still, silent in the face of those who accused him.

Then some said, 'We heard him claim he would destroy the Temple, and build another one in three days, one not of human making!' But even then they couldn't agree.

The High Priest watched Jesus in amazement. 'Haven't you got anything to say for yourself? Have you heard what they are saying about you?' But Jesus returned his gaze, saying nothing. Then the High Priest asked a question, the one they had all been leading towards.

'Are you the Messiah, the Christ, the Son of God?' The chamber fell silent. All eyes turned to Jesus.

'I am,' said Jesus. The High Priest raged, ripping his clothes, horrified at what he was hearing.

'He's claiming to be the Son of God! This is blasphemy – he has condemned himself!'

They all began to spit on Jesus, and mock him. And the guards took him away to be beaten. By first light, they had decided to hand him over to the governor, Pilate, who had the power to sentence him to death.

The Roman Governor

MARK 15:1–20

THE CHIEF PRIESTS, teachers and religious leaders led the bound Jesus to Pilate, the Roman governor of their occupied country. Pilate questioned him.

'Are you the king of the Jews?'

'Yes, it is as you say,' Jesus replied. Then the chief priests began a furious rain of accusations. But Jesus was still, saying nothing.

'Aren't you going to answer them? They are accusing you of so much!' But Jesus did not answer. Pilate was astonished by his silence. He had seen many prisoners in his time, but never one like this.

It was the custom to release a prisoner at the Passover, and the crowd came to ask Pilate to do so again. Pilate asked them, 'Shall I set free the king of the Jews?'

'We want Barabbas!' they yelled, stirred up by the chief priests. Barabbas was a rebel, and a murderer.

'What shall I do with the one you call the king of the Jews?'

'Crucify him!' they shouted.

'Why? What has he done wrong?' Pilate's voice was powerful, but the mob roared, 'Crucify him!'

And so Barabbas was set free, and Pilate handed Jesus over to the soldiers.

They took him to the governor's palace, and the whole garrison came out to see him. They knew he was accused of being 'the king of the Jews', and so they dressed him in a mockery of royal robes. They draped a fine purple cloth over his shoulders and wove together a crown of piercing thorns, which they pressed down onto his head. They called out, 'Hail, king of the Jews!' Some struck him with a stick, and spat on him, while others laughed and bowed low before him. Then they took off the purple robe, put his own clothes back on him and led him away to crucify him.

The only crown Jesus ever wore was the mock crown of thorns. It is a reminder to Christians that Jesus came to offer hope to those who suffer.

'It is Finished'

JOHN 19:17–34

Because of Jesus' crucifixion, the cross has become the most important symbol of the Christian faith.

JESUS CARRIED HIS CROSS TO "The Place of the Skull', or 'Golgotha' in Hebrew. Here, the soldiers crucified him with two others: one on each side.

Above his head they hung a notice prepared by Pilate. It was written in Hebrew, Latin and Greek, so that all could understand it. It said:

JESUS OF NAZARETH, KING OF THE JEWS

But the chief priest objected. 'It should say he *claimed* to be king, not that he *was* king!'

'What I've written, I've written!' Pilate replied.

The soldiers began to divide up Jesus' clothes between them, but they could not share his robe because it was made of one seamless piece of cloth. So, at the foot of the cross, they played a game of dice, with the robe as a prize.

Nearby huddled a group of women. Mary, Jesus' mother, was there, with her sister. Mary, the wife of Clopas, and Mary Magdalene were with them, as was John.

Jesus spoke to his mother. 'Dear woman, here is your son!' And he said to John, 'Here is your mother!'

From that day, John took her into his home, caring for her as his own mother.

Then, knowing that all was complete, and the work was done, Jesus said, 'I am thirsty!' He was given sour wine on a sponge to drink. Then he said, 'It is finished,' and bowed his head, giving up his spirit to death.

Because the sabbath was near, they agreed to hurry the deaths. And so the soldiers came, and broke the legs of the man on one side, and on the other. When they came to Jesus, he was already dead, and they pierced his side with a spear. Blood and water flowed from it.

Burial, Guards and Resurrection

MATTHEW
27:57 – 28:8

THE DAY OF JESUS' CRUCIFIXION was coming to an end, and Joseph, a rich man from Arimathea, hurried to see Pilate.

'Sir,' Joseph said, 'I come to request my Master's body for burial.' And Pilate agreed.

Joseph took the body and wrapped it carefully in a clean linen cloth. Then he laid the body in his own tomb — one that had been freshly cut out of a rock. He had a heavy stone rolled across the entrance, and left.

Mary Magdalene and the other Mary were nearby, keeping faithful watch.

The next day, Pilate received more visitors: chief priests and religious leaders.

'You have come to see me about Jesus of Nazareth, I suppose?' he asked. 'Sir,' they replied, 'while he was alive, Jesus claimed he would rise again after three days. We suggest you place a guard on the tomb.'

'Take a guard, and seal the tomb as well as you possibly can!' Pilate answered uneasily. And so they did.

At first light on Sunday, after the sabbath, Mary Magdalene and the other Mary hurried to the tomb. They felt the ground shake and tremble beneath them, and an angel appeared, shining with brightness as searing as lightning, wearing clothes as dazzling as snow. The angel rolled the stone away, while the guards could only cower and quail, falling to the ground in terror.

The angel spoke to the women. 'Don't be afraid! You are looking for Jesus – but he is risen! Here is the empty space where he lay! Give this message to the others: he is going to Galilee, where you will see him.'

The women set off at a run, wide-eyed with joy and terror, to find the other disciples and tell them the angel's words.

'I Have Seen the Lord!'

JOHN 20:11–18

MARY MAGDALENE STOOD OUTSIDE the tomb, weeping, as she had wept at the foot of the cross. It was now the third day since Jesus' death, and darkness trembled at the first touch of morning light. But still, Mary wept.

Bent low with grief, she looked into the tomb, and there, she saw two figures, angels in white, seated where the body should have been.

'Woman, why do you weep?' they asked her.

'They have taken my Lord away,' she replied, 'and I don't know where they have put him!' As she said this she turned away from the tomb. There was a figure standing in front of her, but her eyes were blurred with tears, and she did not know that it was Jesus.

'Woman, why do you weep? Who is it you are looking for?' Mary thought he must be the gardener, working in the cool of the early morning.

'Sir, if you have taken him away, please tell me, so I can go and bring him back!'

But Jesus simply said, 'Mary!' When she heard him calling her name, she looked up, and knew it was Jesus.

'*Rabboni!*' she cried, which means 'teacher'.

Then Jesus said, 'Mary, don't cling to me so. I have not yet gone to the Father. Go and tell the brothers: "I am going back to my Father and your Father, to my God and your God."'

So she ran back, and told them everything that had happened, saying, 'I have seen the Lord!'

Mary Magdalene was one of several women named in the Gospels who were devoted followers of Jesus. She came from the town of Magdala.

On the Road to Emmaus

LUKE 24:13–35

IT WAS THE THIRD DAY AFTER the crucifixion, and two of Jesus' followers decided to leave the city for Emmaus, about eleven kilometres away. They had heard the story the women brought back from the tomb – that Jesus had risen – but could it really be true?

As they walked, they talked about all that had happened, trying to make sense of it. A third person joined them, but they did not recognize that it was Jesus.

'What are you talking about so intently?' he asked. They stopped, their faces dull with sadness. Cleopas, one of the two, said, 'Haven't you heard what's been going on in Jerusalem?'

'Tell me.'

'Jesus of Nazareth, the prophet full of God's power, was betrayed and crucified – and our hope died with him. We were so sure he was the one who would save us. But this morning, some of the women astounded us. They went to the tomb very early, but came running back with fire in their eyes, saying the tomb was empty, and angels had told them he was alive again!'

'Don't you understand?' Jesus asked. 'Haven't you read all those prophecies? They all tell of how the Messiah, God's chosen one, had to suffer and then rise again!' And – starting with Moses and working his

way through – he showed them how the holy writings pointed to him.

They arrived in Emmaus, but Jesus carried on walking.

'Stay with us – it's getting dark!' So Jesus stayed, and sat down at their table. Then he picked up the bread, blessed it, broke it and handed it to them. And at that moment, in the breaking of the bread, their eyes opened. They knew it was Jesus. Then he disappeared.

They turned to each other. 'When he spoke, could you feel your heart burning inside you?' And they rushed back to Jerusalem, longing to rejoice with their friends.

Seeing and Believing

JOHN 20:19–31

IT WAS THE EVENING OF THE third day, and some of Jesus' followers were hiding away behind locked doors, fearing that the religious leaders would turn on them, too. But Jesus came to them, and stood as one with them.

'Peace be with you!' he greeted them. The disciples' fear melted away – their hearts were lit up with joy, and their laughter filled the room.

But one of the disciples had not been with them. It was Thomas, sometimes called Didymus or the Twin. And they told him what had happened when they met him next. 'We have seen the Lord!' they said. But Thomas thought they were gabbling nonsense.

'Unless I see those nail marks in his hands, put my finger where the nails were, and put my hand to his pierced side, I will not believe a word of it!' he said.

A week later, they were all together, including Thomas, when Jesus came to them again, though the doors were locked. 'Peace be with you!' he said. Then he turned to Thomas.

'Put your finger here, see my hands. Reach out to my side. Stop doubting, and believe!'

'My Lord, and my God!' Thomas replied, trembling with awe.

'You believe because you have seen with your own eyes. Blessed are those who have not seen, but still believe!'

John, who wrote down an account of Jesus' life, explained why he did so like this. 'Jesus did many more wonderful things that are not written down here. But these are written so that you will believe that Jesus is the Christ, the Son of God. And because you believe, you may have abundant, overflowing life.'

'Peter, Do You Love Me?'

JOHN 21:1–19

In this story, Peter declares his faithfulness to Jesus three times. Christians see this as making up for the three times he denied knowing Jesus at the time of the trial.

A GROUP OF JESUS' FOLLOWERS had returned to the shores of the Sea of Galilee. Thomas, Simon Peter and John were among them.

Suddenly, Simon Peter jumped up. 'I'm going fishing!'

'We'll come too!' said the others. Simon Peter uncovered his old boat, and pushed it out into the water. All night they fished, but they caught nothing. Then, as the morning sun gleamed on the empty decks, Jesus called to them from the shore, but they didn't recognize him.

'Good morning! Did you catch anything?'

'No!'

'Try throwing the nets down on the right-hand side of the boat.' They did what he said, and immediately, the nets were heavy with enormous, wriggling fish. The fishermen heaved on the ropes, but they couldn't pull in the net. Then John said, 'It's the Master!' Simon Peter looked up, and a wide smile spread across his face. He dived into the water, swimming strongly to the shore. The others followed by boat, dragging the net behind them.

'Bring some fish over here!' Jesus said, and they saw he had a fire burning. Jesus made a breakfast of loaves and fish, and he gave it to them. They sat there, eating hungrily. No one dared ask, 'Who are you?' They knew it was Jesus.

When they had eaten, Jesus turned to Simon Peter, and searched his eyes. They had not yet spoken of the night Simon Peter denied him three times.

'Simon, son of John, do you love me?'

'Yes, Master, you know I love you!'

'Feed my lambs.'

He asked again, 'Simon, son of John, do you love me?'

'Yes, Master, you know I love you!'
'Take care of my flock.'
He asked a third time: 'Simon, son of John, do you love me?'
'Master, you know everything! You must know I love you!'
'Feed my sheep. And come, follow me.'

Taken Up to Heaven

LUKE 24:36–53,
ACTS 1:8–11

Jesus' being taken up into heaven is often called the Ascension.

THE DISCIPLES TALKED AND TALKED about all that had happened – how Jesus was not dead, but alive. Then, as they were talking, they saw that Jesus himself was standing with them. They took a step back, startled, but he reassured them:

'Peace be with you! Don't be afraid or be full of questions and doubts. I'm real – not a ghost! Look at my hands and feet – touch and see. I'm flesh and blood.' And he showed them his hands and feet.

But the disciples just stood dumbstruck.

'Have you anything to eat?' Jesus asked gently, and they quickly gave him some cooked fish.

'Now do you understand the things I told you? And all the things that have been written in the holy books?' As he explained it all to them, their minds began to open.

'It is written that the Christ, the chosen one of God, had to suffer, and rise again on the third day. Because of this, forgiveness, and new life, is on offer to all people. And your job is to tell everyone what you have seen and heard – start in Jerusalem, and then spread the message to the ends of the earth. But not yet. For now, wait in Jerusalem, and the Spirit will come to give you such power!'

As he blessed them, he was taken up before their eyes, and hidden in a cloud. They were staring up after him, but then noticed two figures in white standing with them. 'Why are you looking up into the sky?' they asked. 'This Jesus, who was taken from you into heaven, will one day come back the same way!'

And all Jesus' followers were overflowing with joy. They returned to Jerusalem, filling the Temple with praises to God, and waiting for the coming of the Spirit.

A Mighty Wind, and Tongues of Flame

ACTS 2:1–19, 42–47

Pentecost is celebrated in the Christian church as the time was God sent the Holy Spirit to strengthen and encourage the followers of Jesus. They believe the Holy Spirit strengthens and encourages all Christians everywhere.

IT WAS THE FEAST OF PENTECOST, and all of Jerusalem was waking up to a day of celebration and joy. It was time to give thanks for the barley harvest, for the fruitfulness of the grain.

The disciples were together in one house when suddenly the sound of a rushing, mighty wind burst on them, shaking the house, tugging at their clothes and their hair. The wind was pouring down from heaven itself. Then came fire, which separated so that each of them had tongues of flame resting on them, shining brightly without burning them. All were filled with the Holy Spirit, and began talking in other tongues.

'What's going on?' people said. 'We can hear our own languages spoken, even though we come from many countries!'

Peter talked to the crowd. 'This is the gift we were promised by the prophet, Joel. "I will pour out my Spirit on everyone. All will prophesy, all will have visions and dreams – men and women, young and old alike. All will see wonders from heaven itself, and all who come to God will be saved!"'

So on that day, thousands believed, and joined those who had followed Jesus by the Sea of Galilee. They lived together in joy and awe, sharing food, and giving thanks. And every day more people believed.

Where Jesus Lived

THE LAND WHERE JESUS LIVED is on the eastern shore of the Mediterranean Sea.

People grew crops that thrived in the warm, dry summers — crops such as olives, grapes, barley and vegetables. Shepherds led their flocks of sheep and goats to graze the hillsides and cattle were carefully raised on lusher pastures. Many of Jesus' teachings refer to everyday activites such as these.

Jesus' birth is described as being in **Bethlehem**. This was the same place where, hundreds of years earlier, the nation's great king David had been born. It is something that identifies Jesus as the true successor to David.

Jerusalem was the city claimed by David as his capital. It was also where David's son, Solomon, first built a Temple. In the time of Jesus, a glittering new Temple had been built on the orders of the local king, Herod the Great.

Jesus himself was raised in the region of Galilee, in the town of **Nazareth**. When the local people rejected him as a teacher, he moved to **Capernaum**, a fishing village on the shore of **Lake Galilee**, also known as the Sea of Galilee. Most of his teaching took place in the towns and villages around Galilee, although on several occasions he travelled south to **Jericho** and Jerusalem. It was just outside the city walls that he was crucified.

MEDITERRANEAN SEA

Caesarea Philippi

Capernaum

GALILEE

Lake Galilee

Magdala

Cana

Nazareth

SAMARIA

RIVER JORDAN

JUDEA

Jerusalem

Bethany

Jericho

Bethlehem

DEAD SEA

Index